W9-ADQ-656

COVER

FELIX KLEE COLL., BERNE 1939

THE PICTURE "WITH GREEN STOCK-INGS" REPRODUCED ON THE FRONT OF THIS BOOK, SHOWS HOW A MASTER PAINTER CAN TELL A COMPLETE STORY WITH A FEW LINES. A LITTLE GIRL WITH LONG RED HAIR, A GREEN BALL, AND GREEN STOCKINGS IS PLAYING OUTDOORS. THE GOLDEN SUN IS REFLECTED ON HER ARMS, IN THE AIR AROUND HER AND UPON THE GROUND. ABOVE HER HEAD ARE BLUE PATCHES OF SKY AND A HINT OF THE SUN ITSELF AT THE TOP OF HER LEFT ARM.
THE ∪ SHAPED BY HER ARMS IS REPEATED IN THE LINES OF HER SKIRT.

FORGETFUL ANGEL, 1939 KLEE-STIFTUNG, BERNE

BARBARIAN CAPTAIN   FELIX KLEE COLLECTION, BERNE

DEDICATED TO MY WIFE, INA ANDERS RABOFF

COPYRIGHT © ARS, N.Y./ADAGP 1988
ALL RIGHTS RESERVED. NO PART OF THIS BOOK MAY BE USED OR REPRODUCED IN ANY MANNER WHATSOEVER
WITHOUT WRITTEN PERMISSION EXCEPT IN THE CASE OF BRIEF QUOTATIONS EMBODIED IN CRITICAL ARTICLES
AND REVIEWS. PRINTED IN THE UNITED STATES OF AMERICA. PACKAGED BY LRN COMPANY. FOR INFORMATION
ADDRESS J.B. LIPPINCOTT JUNIOR BOOKS, 10 EAST 53RD STREET, NEW YORK, N.Y. 10022. PUBLISHED SIMULTANEOUSLY
IN CANADA BY FITZHENRY & WHITESIDE LIMITED, TORONTO.

LIBRARY OF CONGRESS CATALOGING-IN-PUBLICATION DATA
RABOFF, ERNEST LLOYD
    PAUL KLEE
    (ART FOR CHILDREN)
REPRINT. ORIGINALLY PUBLISHED: GARDEN CITY, N.Y. : DOUBLEDAY, 1968. SUMMARY: A BRIEF BIOGRAPHY OF PAUL KLEE ACCOMPANIES FOURTEEN
COLOR REPRODUCTIONS AND CRITICAL INTERPRETATIONS OF HIS WORKS. 1. KLEE, PAUL, 1879-1940-CRITICISM AND INTERPRETATION - JUVENILE
LITERATURE. 2. PAINTING, GERMAN - JUVENILE LITERATURE. 3. PAINTING, MODERN - 20TH CENTURY - GERMANY - JUVENILE LITERATURE. [1. KLEE,
PAUL, 1879-1940. 2. ARTISTS. 3. PAINTING, GERMAN. 4. PAINTING, MODERN - GERMANY. 5. ART APPRECIATION] I. KLEE, PAUL, 1879-1940.
II. TITLE. III. SERIES: ART FOR CHILDREN.
ND 588.K5R3   1988   759.3   [92]   87-16864   ISBN 0-397-32226-7

PAUL KLEE

By Ernest Raboff

Library
St. Josephs College
Patchogue, N. Y. 11772

ART
FOR
CHILDREN

J. B. LIPPINCOTT · NEW YORK

PAUL KLEE WAS BORN IN

SWITZERLAND ON DECEMBER 18, 1879. HIS
FATHER HANS WAS A MUSIC TEACHER AND HIS
MOTHER IDA MARIA LIKED TO DRAW.

PAUL KLEE BECAME A VIOLINIST AND AN ARTIST.

AS A CHILD, HE LOVED CATS, AND THROUGHOUT HIS
LIFE HE CONTINUED TO DRAW AND PAINT THEM.
HIS FAVORITE CAT WAS BIMBO.

THIS ARTIST WAS A SERIOUS STUDENT WHO
MASTERED MANY LANGUAGES, HISTORIES, AND SCIENCES.
HE WAS ALSO A FINE WRITER
AND TEACHER. HE WAS ADMIRED
AND RESPECTED BY ALL OF THE
FAMOUS PEOPLE HE KNEW
AND WHO KNEW OF HIM.

PAUL KLEE WAS
A WORKING ARTIST.
WHEN HE DIED AT
SIXTY YEARS OF AGE
IN 1940, HE LEFT AT
LEAST 8926
WORKS OF ART.

DRAWING OF PAUL KLEE BY THE AUTHOR

PAUL KLEE PAINTED THIS WATERCOLOR,
"THE NIESEN", FOLLOWING A TRIP TO NORTH AFRICA
IN 1914. AFTERWARD HE SAID, "I AM POSSESSED
BY COLOR...IT WILL POSSESS ME FOREVER.

I AND COLOR ARE ONE. I AM A PAINTER."

THE BLUE PYRAMID PUSHES ITS NOSE INTO THE SKY.

THE SIDES STRETCH OUT
LIKE PROTECTING ARMS.

THE MULTI-COLORED
SQUARES LOOK LIKE
BUILDING BLOCKS
SPARKLING IN THE HOT
SAND UNDER THE BLAZ-
ING SUN.

THE MANY DIFFERENT
SHAPES SURROUND THE
PYRAMID AS THOUGH
THEY WERE A GROUP
OF PEOPLE LISTENING
TO EVERY WORD OF
THIS ANCIENT, WISE,
PATIENT AND IMPRES-
SIVE PROPHET.

ANTIQUE FIGURE 1940 KLEE-STIFTUNG, BERNE

THE TREE HOUSE   1918   PASADENA ART MUSEUM

WHO WOULD NOT WANT TO HAVE "A TREE HOUSE" LIKE PAUL KLEE'S? WHAT A MAGNIFICENT TREE. ON IT ARE BUILT LADDERS THAT REACH FROM THE GROUND, UP AND AROUND THE TRUNK, TO LITTLE HOUSES SET ON THE BRANCHES. SOMEONE IS STANDING AT THE BOTTOM OF THE LADDER WITH ONE HAND ON IT, READY TO CLIMB.

WHEN YOU LIVE IN A TREE HOUSE, YOU ARE HIGH IN THE SKY. THE BIRDS FLYING PAST YOUR DOOR ARE SO CLOSE YOU CAN ALMOST COUNT THE FEATHERS ON THEIR WIDESPREAD WINGS AND THE SPOTS ON THEIR BODIES.

A TREE HOUSE IS A GOOD PLACE TO WATCH THE SUNSET TURN ALL THE SKY A BRILLIANT RED.

AT NIGHT TIME THE STARS ARE SO BIG THAT THEY SEEM TO HANG LIKE SPARKLING CHRISTMAS TREE ORNAMENTS.

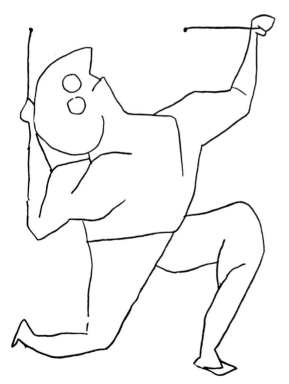

FORMER KETTLE DRUMMER, 1940

PAUL KLEE

WROTE: "IT IS NOT MY TASK TO REPRODUCE APPEARANCES... FOR THAT THERE IS THE PHOTOGRAPHIC PLATE.

I WANT TO PENETRATE TO THE INMOST MEANING OF THE MODEL.

I WANT TO REACH THE HEART.

I WRITE WORDS ON THE FOREHEADS AND ROUND THE LIPS. BUT MY FACES ARE TRUER THAN LIFE."

"ART

DOES NOT REPRODUCE THE VISIBLE. IT RENDERS IT VISIBLE."

"IN THIS WAY WE LEARN TO LOOK BEYOND THE SURFACE AND GET TO THE ROOTS OF THINGS."

FALL 1938 KLEE-STIFTUNG, BERNE

THE NIESEN 1915 WATERCOLOR, H. RUPF COLLECTION, BERNE

"MAID OF SAXONY" IS AN EXCELLENT EXAMPLE OF THE USE OF SIMPLE LINES AND STRONG COLORS TO CREATE A PAINTING THAT REVEALS MORE EACH TIME IT IS STUDIED.

THE YOUNG GIRL HAS BRIGHT ORANGE HAIR. PAUL KLEE PAINTS HER WITH CURVING LINES AND THE SIMPLE ROUNDED FORMS OF YOUTH.

AFRICAN VILLAGE SCENE   1925

HER GREEN EYES MATCH THE COLOR OF HER BLOUSE. THEY ARE SET FAR APART AND ARE WIDE OPEN TO SEE ALL THE WORLD AROUND HER. SHE HAS A SLIGHT SMILE ON HER FACE AND HER ARMS ARE SWINGING AS SHE WALKS. THE BEAUTIFUL DEEP BLUE SKY IS ALL AROUND HER.

MAID OF SAXONY 1922   PASADENA ART MUSEUM

THE "YOUNG TREE" IS A TENDER AND LOVING WORK. SOFT BRANCHES BEND IN THE LIGHT SPRING SHOWER.

THE PALE BLOSSOMS HANG ON THE ENDS OF THE TWIGS LIKE BUTTONS.

THE PINK BACKGROUND LOOKS FRESH AND NEWBORN. WINTER IS OVER. IT IS TIME FOR ALL YOUNG THINGS TO GO OUT TO PLAY AND GROW IN THE SUN.

EVEN THE BRANCHES ARE RAISING THEMSELVES TOWARD THE SKY.

THE ARTIST REMINDS US HOW WONDERFUL THE SPRING IS.

THE MENAGERIE PARADES 1926

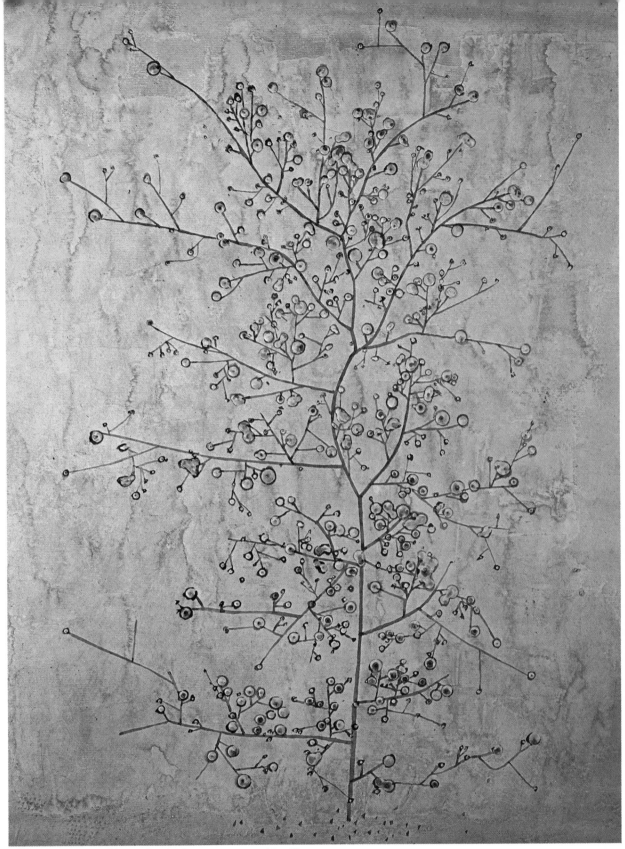

YOUNG TREE 1932 PRIVATE COLLECTION, BERNE

"LANDSCAPE WITH YELLOW BIRDS."
THIS ENTIRE WATERCOLOR IS MADE OF SMILING
LINES... WHICH BECOME GRACEFULLY CURVING
PLANTS.

THE PAINTING IS MADE OF CIRCLES AND HALF-CIRCLES
FORMED BY THE SHAPE OF THE LEAVES. AFTER YOU
LOOK AT THEM FOR A WHILE, THEY SEEM TO BE
MOVING.

THE YELLOW BIRDS MAKE A CIRCLE THAT WE
COMPLETE WITH OUR EYES.

THIS SHOWS US
HOW TO MAKE
MORE CIRCLES
FROM THE SHAPES
OF THE LEAVES
AND BRANCHES.

EVERYTHING CURVES
IN THIS LANDSCAPE.

THERE ARE
NO STRAIGHT LINES
IN NATURE.

SHIPWRECKED 1938   KLEE-STIFTUNG, BERNE

LANDSCAPE WITH YELLOW BIRDS   1923   WATERCOLOR-GOUACHE

"A CHILD'S GAME" IS A PAINTING THAT MOVES ∿.
THE LITTLE GIRL IS RUNNING THROUGH A GARDEN OF
FLOWERS A GOOSE IS AT HER SIDE. ONE OF HER EYES
IS A BALL. THE OTHER EYE IS AN S. THE FIRST ONE
IS TO PLAY WITH—THE
SECOND IS FOR SEEING.

EVEN THE GOOSE
SEEMS TO BE
PLAYING THE
GAME.
PERHAPS
THE LITTLE
GIRL IS
POINTING TO
WHERE ALL
THE FUN IS.

SHE MIGHT
BE GOING
TO THE NEXT
PAGE TO
WATCH THE
BOATS IN
THE
HARBOR.

ANOTHER CAMEL! 1939   F. SCHANG COLLECTION, NEW YORK

LANDSCAPE WITH YELLOW BIRDS   1923   WATERCOLOR-GOUACHE

"A CHILD'S GAME" IS A PAINTING THAT MOVES 〰️. THE LITTLE GIRL IS RUNNING THROUGH A GARDEN OF FLOWERS A GOOSE IS AT HER SIDE. ONE OF HER EYES IS A BALL. THE OTHER EYE IS AN S. THE FIRST ONE IS TO PLAY WITH—THE SECOND IS FOR SEEING.

EVEN THE GOOSE SEEMS TO BE PLAYING THE GAME. PERHAPS THE LITTLE GIRL IS POINTING TO WHERE ALL THE FUN IS.

SHE MIGHT BE GOING TO THE NEXT PAGE TO WATCH THE BOATS IN THE HARBOR.

ANOTHER CAMEL! 1939   F. SCHANG COLLECTION, NEW YORK

"THE FLAGGED TOWN" IS SEEN IN THIS PAINTING
WITH BOTH THE SUN AND THE MOON
IN THE SKY.

OVER THE CITY THE WIND,
BLOWING FIRST FROM ONE DIRECTION AND THEN
FROM THE OTHER, KEEPS THE FLAGS
UNFURLED.

THE BUILDINGS SEEM TO FLOAT IN THE AIR.
HELD UP BY GAY AND BRIGHTLY COLORED BALLOONS.

THE STRUCTURES OF THE CITY ARE ETCHED IN
SILVERY MOONLIGHT AGAINST THE DEEP BLUE
SKY.

EVEN AT NIGHT
THE TOWN,
ALTHOUGH SLEEPING
QUIETLY, IS
GLOWING. THE
FLAGS STAND
GUARD, FULL OF
JOY
AND
LIFE.

ORGELBERG 1934

DEPARTURE OF SHIPS 1927 OIL   W. ALLENBACH COLLECTION, BERNE

PEOPLE ARE ALWAYS GOING AND COMING.

IN THE "DEPARTURE OF SHIPS" THE ARTIST TELLS US THAT EVERY DAY AND NIGHT SOMEWHERE A BOAT IS LEAVING ON A JOURNEY.

UNDER A BLUE MOON, THE VESSELS WITH ORANGE AND RED SAILS FOLLOW THE ARROW TO THE SEA.

HAVE YOU EVER SEEN THE WAY SHADOWS IN THE MOONLIGHT MAKE A CRAZY-QUILT PATTERN?

THE ARTIST SEES AND RECORDS WONDERFUL

MEMORIES

WITH HIS

PAINTS

AND

HIS

BRUSHES.

SAILING SHIPS MOVING GENTLY 1927 PRIVATE COLLECTION, BERNE

A CHILD'S GAME   1939   OIL-TEMPERA   FELIX KLEE COLLECTION, BERNE

FLAGGED TOWN 1927 WATERCOLOR, PRIVATE COLLECTION

THE MAGICIAN STANDING AT THE BOTTOM OF THIS
PAINTING OF "FISH MAGIC", SEEMS TO LOOK IN
TWO DIRECTIONS WHILE JUGGLING FISH, FLOWERS,
VASES, AND BALLS.

NOTICE THE PERSON WEARING THE DUNCE CAP IN
THE LOWER LEFT CORNER. PERHAPS THIS
CHARACTER AND THE MAGICIAN ARE ONLY PUPPET
SKIN DIVERS MOVING IN A STRANGE AND BEAUTIFUL
AQUARIUM.

WE CAN ALMOST IMAGINE A FACE IN THE UPPER LEFT
CORNER. COULD IT BELONG TO THE REAL MAGICIAN?

WHAT WE REALLY SEE IS PAUL KLEE'S UNUSUAL
TALENT AS A PAINTER. IT IS TRULY THE ARTIST'S

FISH
MAGIC.

PORTO-FERRAIO-ELBE 1927 P. HART COLLECTION, U.S.A.

FISH MAGIC   1925   ARENSBERG COLLECTION

"ARAB SONG" IS A TUNE OF THE

DESERT PEOPLE OF ARABIA.

THE VEILED ARAB WOMAN IS FRAMED BY HER
COLORFUL CLOTHING. HER EYES PEER IN HAPPY
WONDER OVER THE TOP OF THE ROSE-PINK VEIL.
HER LONG SMILE ENDS IN A CURVE OVER HER
HEART.

WE CAN ALMOST FEEL THE HOT DESERT AIR
AROUND HER LOOSE, SACK-SHAPED BURNOOSE.
THIS DRESS IS MADE OF THE SAME ROUGH
WOVEN BURLAP ON WHICH PAUL KLEE HAS
PAINTED THE
PICTURE.

EVEN
THE STITCHES
SEWN INTO THE
PAINTING RESEMBLE
THE PRIMITIVE NEEDLE-
WORK OF THE ARABIAN
NOMADS
WHO TRAVEL
THE DESERT.

DONKEY EATING OUT OF HAND, 1937

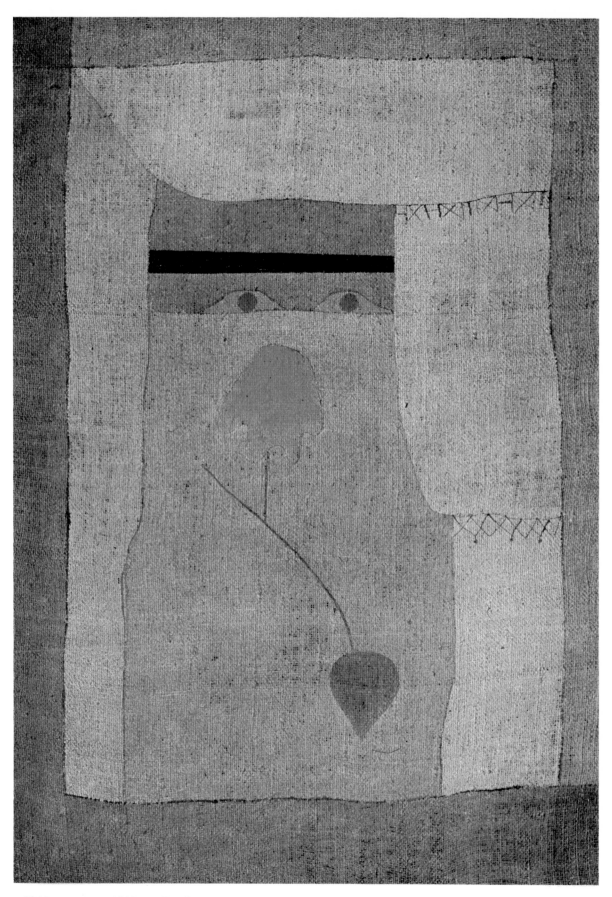

ARAB SONG   1932   THE PHILLIPS GALLERY, WASHINGTON D.C.

"A SHEET OF PICTURES" LOOKS LIKE BOTH A TREASURE HUNTING GAME AND AN ANCIENT STONE CARVING.

PAUL KLEE HAS "CARVED" MANY TREASURES.

THE WOMAN ON THE LEFT RESEMBLES A TEACHER STANDING BEFORE A BLACKBOARD FILLED WITH LARGE AND SMALL DRAWINGS OF SEPARATE OBJECTS.

CAN YOU FIND ANY IN THE PICTURE THAT ARE NOT LISTED HERE?

GLASSES
FISH
A COMB
FIGURES
PENNANTS
STARS
LETTERS
A TABLE
?

NOTICE THAT ALL SEEM TO REVOLVE AROUND THE RED SUN.

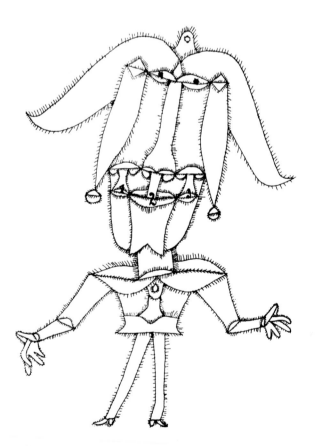

THREE GENTLE WORDS FROM A FOOL , 1925

KNOWN AS "PICTURE ALBUM"   1937   IN THE PHILLIPS GALLERY, WASHINGTON D.C.

SOME PEOPLE SAY THAT FISH IS FOOD FOR THE
BRAIN.

PERHAPS THAT IS WHAT THIS ARTIST MEANT
WHEN HE DREW A LINE FROM THE FISH TO AN
ARROW WHICH POINTS TO A MAN'S HEAD.

PAUL KLEE HAS FILLED HIS PICTURE WITH
OBJECTS AND SYMBOLS
OF LIFE...

MOON   SUN   PLANTS   FISH
AND MAN.

DRAWING FOR "THE SEAFARERS" 1923   KLEE-STIFTUNG, BERNE

AROUND THE FISH 1926 OIL-TEMPERA MUSEUM OF MODERN ART, NEW YORK

REMEMBER PAUL KLEE SAID,

"...LEARN HOW TO LOOK BEYOND THE SURFACE AND GET TO THE ROOTS OF THINGS."

ST. JOSEPH'S COLLEGE - CALLAHAN LIBRARY

3   0 0078709 7

ST. JOSEPH'S COLLEGE - CALLAHAN LIBRARY